SAMSUNG NOTE 3

Your Ultimate User Guide with 100 Tips and Tricks!

DISCLAIMER

Samsung Note 3 is not just a phone and not just a tablet either. If you are reading this user guide, you probably own it and don't know all there is about it.

The Samsung Note 3 is loaded with features, which is what makes it so interesting. There's nothing you cannot do on your Samsung Note 3. From the basic to advanced features, you can operate your phone through voice control or with your palm without touching it! Bet that's not the case in many other phones.

Take clear and crisp pictures, draw sketches or edit images in the most exceptional way possible. Fun with your Samsung Note 3 cannot end.

This user guide will provide you with all the information there is about Samsung Note 3. You will learn about:

- Key features of the phone
- Specifications of various functions
- Applications and features of Samsung Note 3
- A step by step process to use the different features
- Visuals to easily understand the process and functions.

And that's not it, you will also find:

100 tips and tricks which are sure to make the Samsung note 3 fun and easy to use!

Contents

PART 1

Key Specifications

Physical Features

Body dimensions: 151.2 × 79.2 × 8.3mm

Body weight: 168g

Display size: 5.7 inches

Hardware

Processor: 2.3 GHz quad-core Qualcomm Snapdragon 800

Operating system: Android 4.3 with Samsung TouchWiz

Memory

RAM: 3GB

Storage: 32/64GB plus micro SD slot supporting up to 64GB cards

Camera

Back camera: 13-megapixel

Front facing: 2-megapixel

Device Layout

Front View

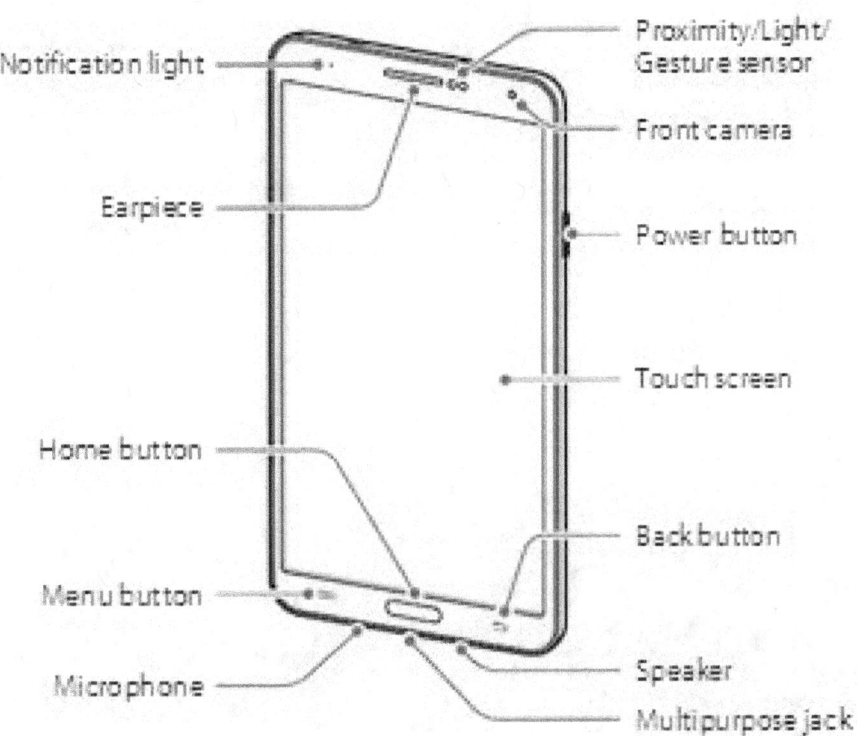

Notification light

Proximity/Light/
Gesture sensor

Front camera

Earpiece

Power button

Touch screen

Home button

Back button

Menu button

Speaker

Microphone

Multipurpose jack

Back View

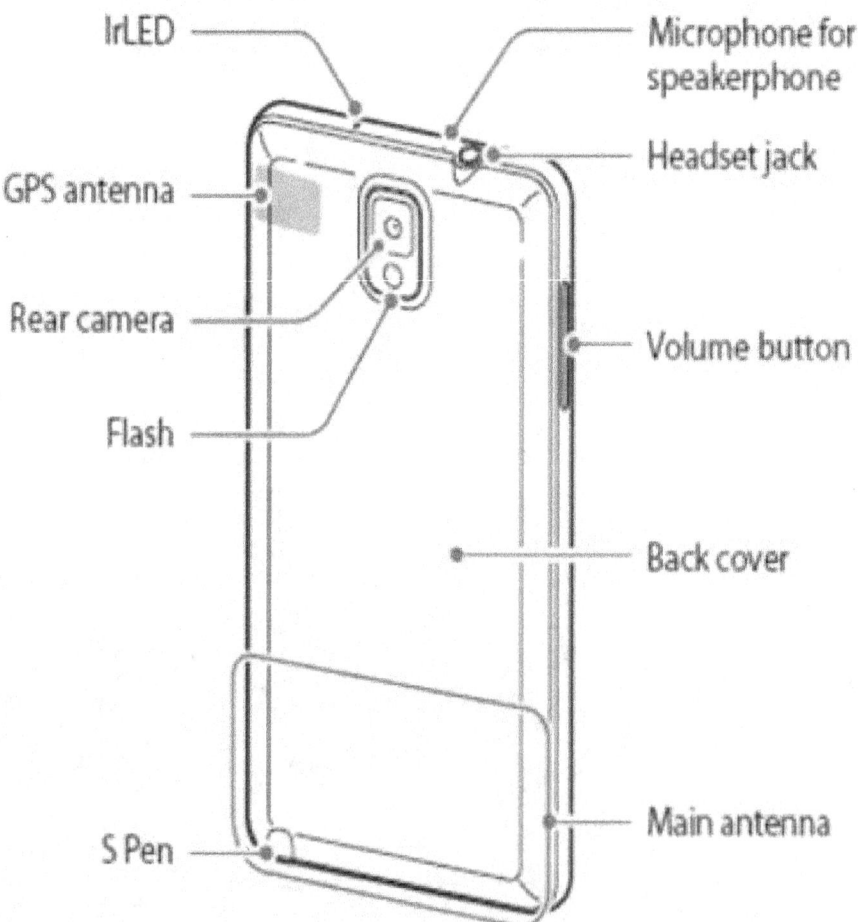

IrLED

Microphone for speakerphone

GPS antenna

Headset jack

Rear camera

Volume button

Flash

Back cover

Main antenna

S Pen

How to Install SIM Card

1. Remove back cover

2. Insert SIM with the golden-colored side facing downwards

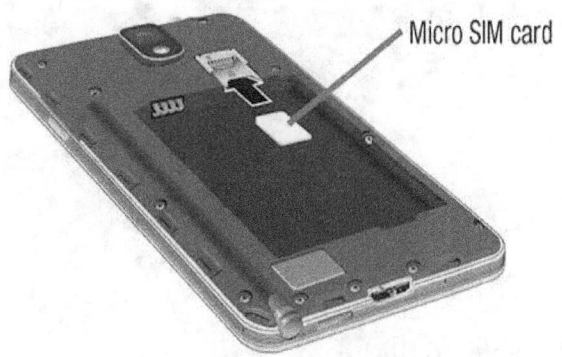

3. Insert in slot until it fixes in place

4. Replace the battery

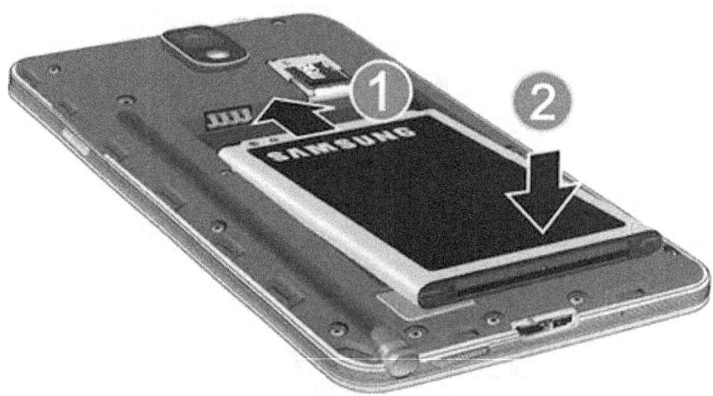

5. Replace back cover

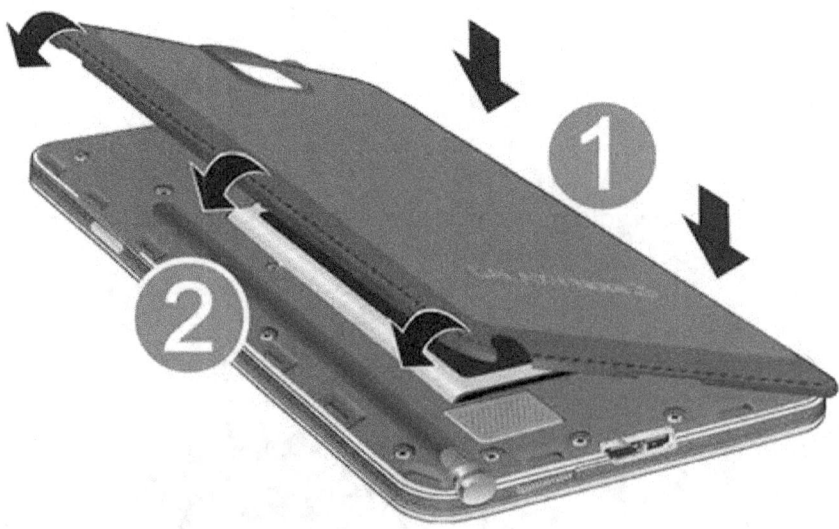

Note: this phone uses a micro SIM card

Removing SIM CARD

To remove the SIM card simply:

1. Remove the back cover and battery
2. Press the SIM gently to pull it

Inserting Memory Card

1. Remove the cover

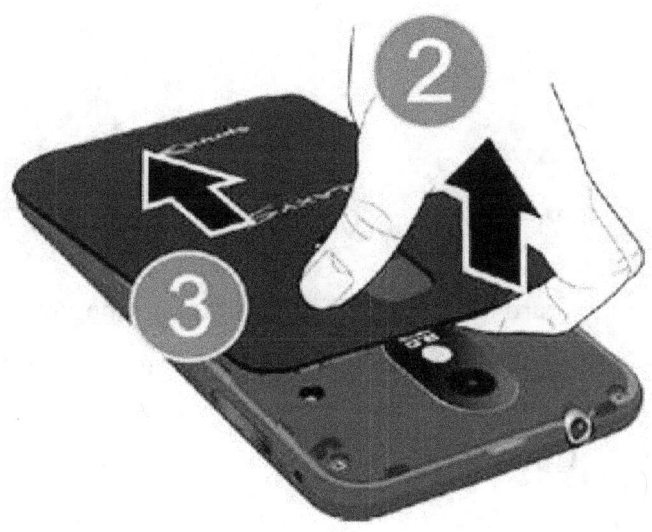

2. Insert memory card until it is secured in card slot

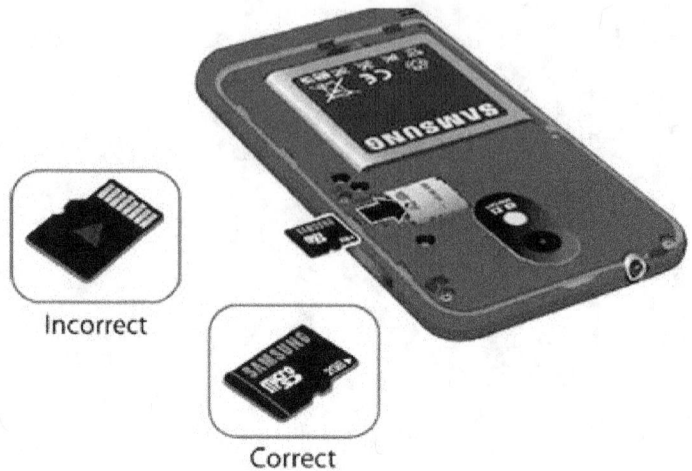

Incorrect

Correct

3. Replace the cover

Removing Memory Card

4. To remove the memory card be sure to safely un-mount it before,

5. Go to apps ⟶ Setting ⟶ General ⟶ Storage ⟶ Un-mount SD card

Formatting Memory Card

1. It is safe to format memory card on device rather than on your computer, otherwise it will not be compatible

2. Go to Apps ⟶ Settings ⟶ General ⟶ Storage ⟶ Format SD card ⟶ erase everything

Charging Battery

To charge your phone, connect the USB with the multipurpose jack.

The phone can be charged with a USB 2.0 or USB 3.0

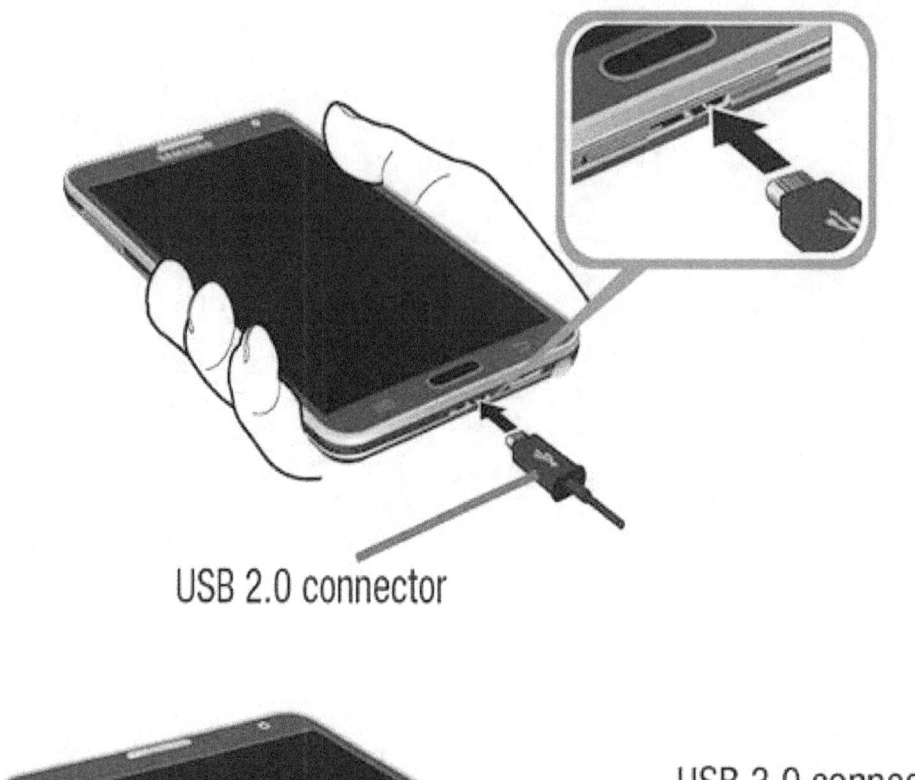

USB 2.0 connector

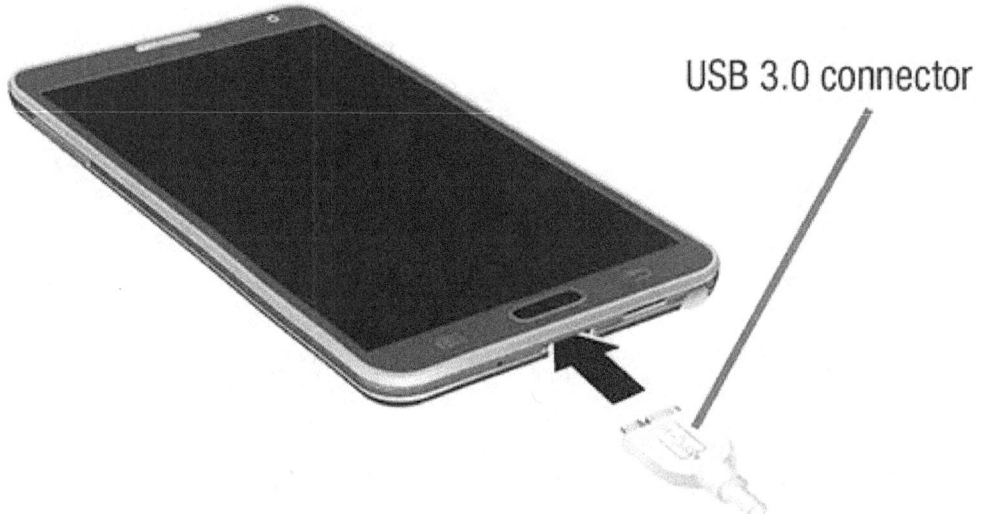

USB 3.0 connector

It can be charged from an electric socket or through the laptop.

When the phone is being charged while turned off, the battery charge status is depicted by the following icons:

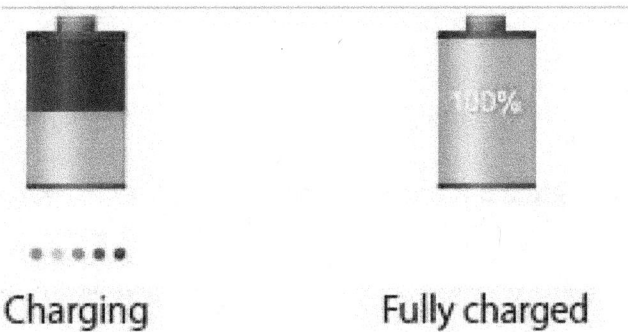

Charging   Fully charged

Touch Control

Tap

Tap the screen to:

6. Open an application

7. Select menu item

8. Press on-screen button

9. Enter a character using the on-screen keyboard

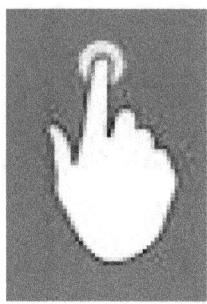

Tap and Hold

Access available options by tapping and holding an icon for more than 2 seconds

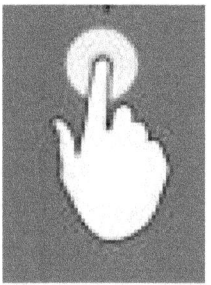

Drag

Tap and hold, and drag an icon, thumbnail or preview to the target or new position

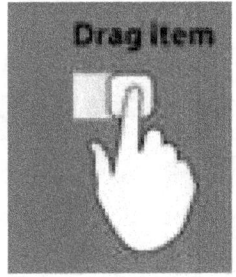

Double-Tap

Double tap to zoom in an image or webpage. To return, double tap again

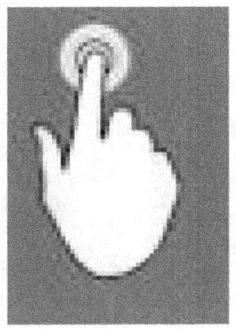

Flick

To view another panel on the home screen or applications screen, flick left or right

To scroll through a webpage or contact list, flick up or down

Pinch

To zoom in an image, webpage or map spread two fingers apart on it

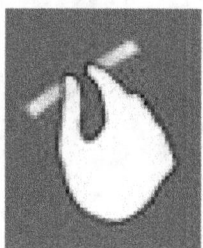

Motion Control

You can control Samsung Note 3 via simple motions.

To activate the motion feature:

Tap Apps——▶ Settings ——▶ Controls——▶ Motions; drag the motions switch to right to enable.

Rotate Screen

Rotating the device automatically adjusts the display to new screen orientation.

To prevent automatic rotation, you can deselect Screen rotation from the notifications panel.

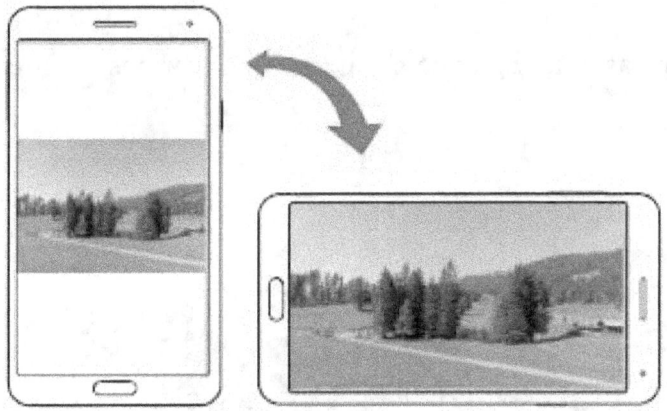

Using S Pen

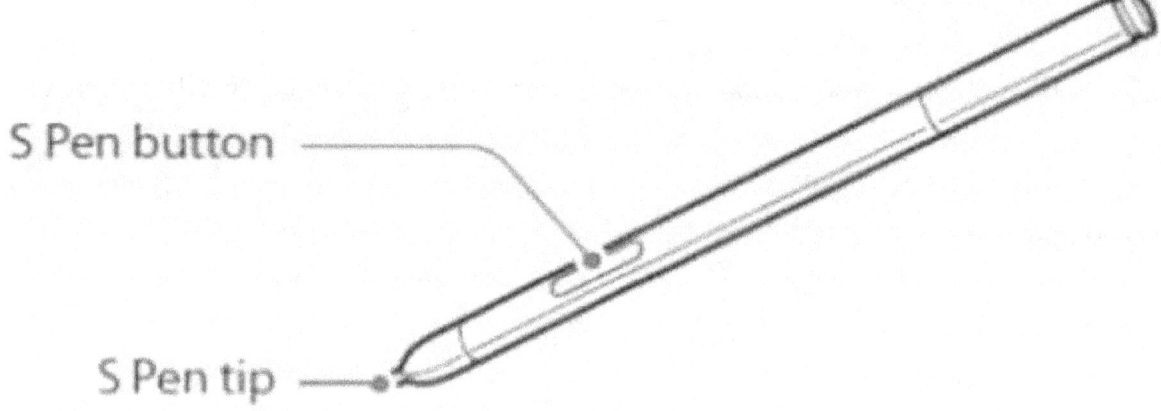

Using the S Pen makes it easier to select items and perform various functions. To use the S Pen pull it out of the slot.

Note: keep the S pen perpendicular to touch screen for best results. Avoid using at sharp angles. The nib of S Pen is also replaceable. You can easily replace it when it gets dull.

Notifications

The notification icon reports missed calls, new messages, calendar events, device status and more. It appears on the status bar at the top of the screen. To open the notifications panel, drag it down from the status bar. To see additional alerts, scroll the list. Drag the bar up which is at the bottom of the screen to close the notifications panel.

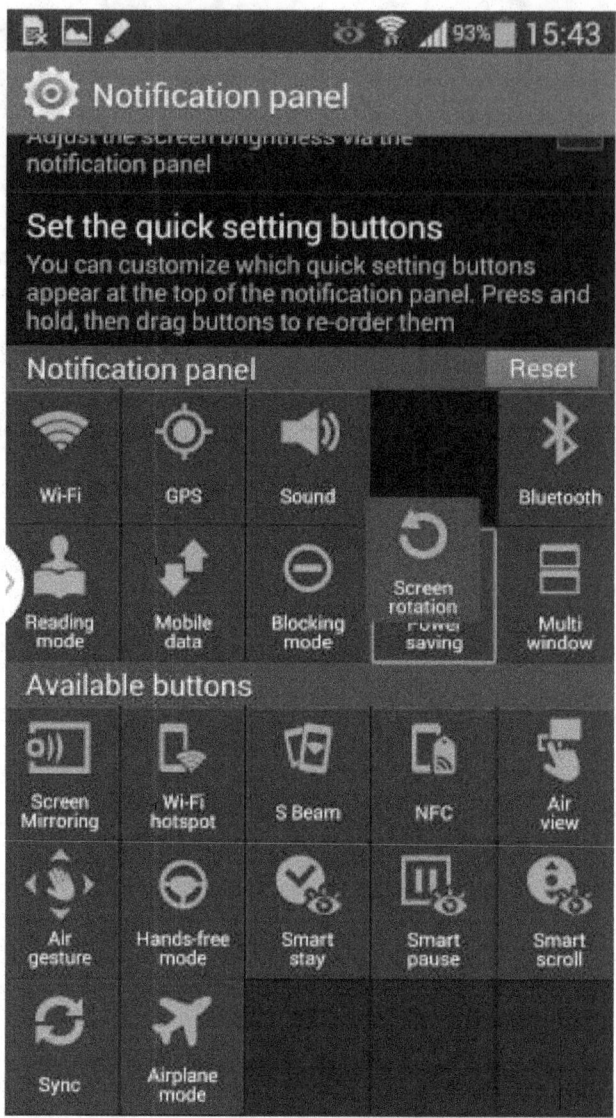

Home Screen

The home screen displays indicator icons, widgets, shortcut icons to applications and more. It is the starting point to access all the features of the device.

You can have multiple panels on the home screen. Scroll left or right to view other panels.

To Change Mode of Home Screen

You can switch between standard and easy mode for the home screen. To enable easy mode:

Tap Apps ⟶ Settings ⟶ Device ⟶ Easy mode ⟶ and drag the switch to right

To Rearrange Items

Add an application

Tap an application icon and hold it, and drag it into panel preview

Add an item

You can add widgets folders or panels to customize the homes screen

Select one of the following categories by tapping and holding the empty area on the home screen:

1. Apps and widgets
2. Folder
3. Page

Move an item

1. Drag an item to a new location by tapping and holding it.
2. Drag it to the side of the screen to move it to another panel.

Remove an item

1. To remove an item, drag it to the rubbish pin that appears at the top of home screen.
2. Release the item when the bin turns red.

Set Wallpaper

1. Tap and hold any empty space on home screen

2. Select set wallpaper

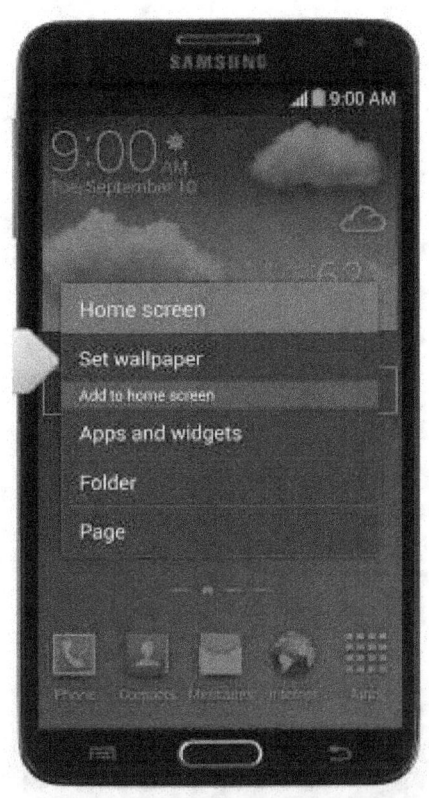

3. Select home screen

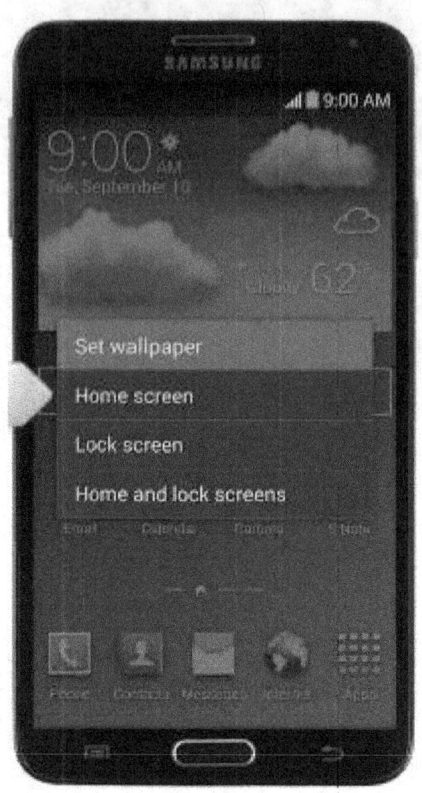

4. Choose wallpaper from gallery, live wallpapers, or wallpapers

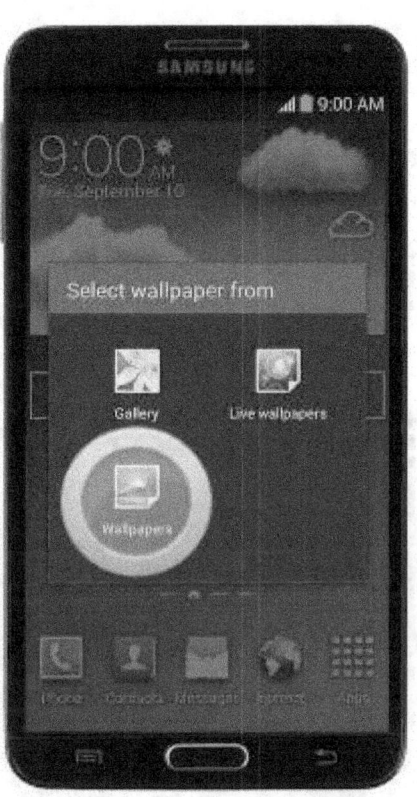

5. Select an image and tap set wallpaper

6. Or you can resize the selected image by dragging the frame

7. Tap done to complete action

Adding and Using Widgets

Widgets provide convenience and information on the home screen. Add widgets to the home screen from the widgets panels to use them.

To add:

1. Tap Apps ⟶ Widgets
2. On the widgets panel scroll left or right
3. To add a widget to home screen, tap and hold it
4. Put it in the location you want
5. To save the location tap anywhere on the screen

Lock and Unlock Device

You can prevent unwanted use and operation of your device through the locked screen

To lock

By pressing the power button the screen turns off and the device goes into lock mode. It gets locked automatically if not used for a particular time.

To unlock

Press the power button

Within the unlock screen area at lower part of screen, flick your finger in any direction.

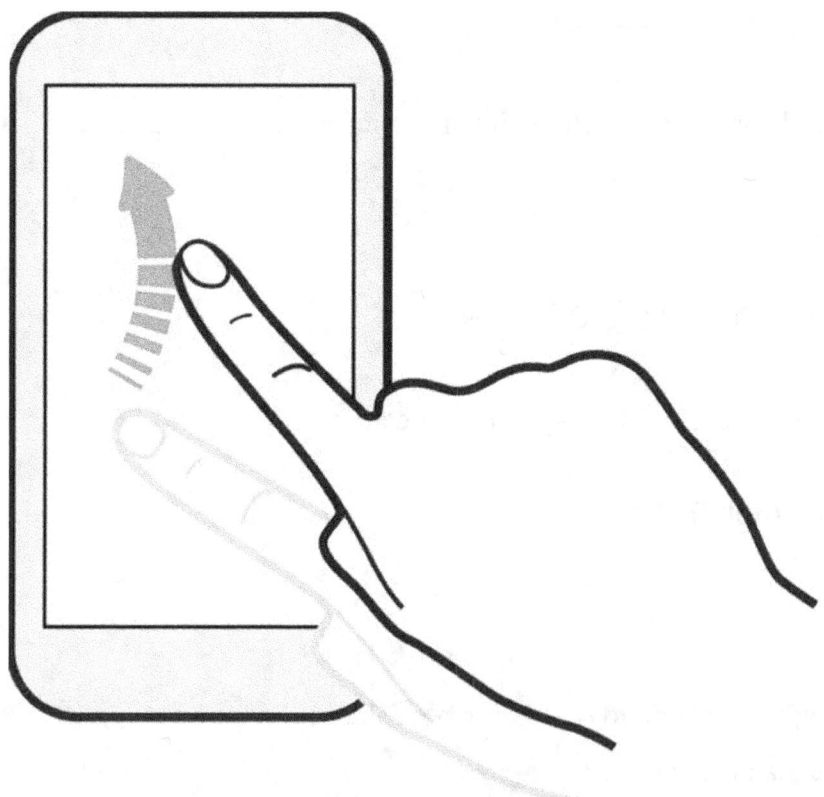

Using Applications

You can use many kinds of applications on the Samsung Note 3 ranging from games to internet applications.

To open application

1. Simply select the application icon on the applications screen to open it
2. Top open an application from recently –used applications
3. To open list of recently used applications, press and hold the home button
4. Select an icon to open it

To close an application

1. Press and hold home button
2. To close the app, tap End next to the application

3. Tap end all to close all running applications.

Note: closing unused applications help maintain device performance and saves battery

Rearrange applications

1. Tap and hold empty home screen area
2. Select edit
3. Tap and hold application to drag to new location

Organize applications in folders

1. Tap empty home screen area
2. Tap edit
3. Tap and hold application to drag to Create folder
4. Enter folder name and tap OK

Installing and uninstalling applications

You can install applications from the Samsung apps store

To uninstall:

1. Tap empty screen area on home screen and select uninstall app
2. Select the desired application to uninstall

Managing Contacts

To enter contact information tap:

To edit a contact tap:

Setting Speed Dial

1. Go to speed dial setting
2. Select speed dial number

3. Select contact for the specific number

To search a contact:

1. You can search a contact by scrolling up or down the contact list
2. Enter search criteria at top of contact list in the search field

Import and export contacts:

1. In the contacts menu, go to import/export
2. Import from SIM card
3. Import from SD card or
4. Import from USB

To export contacts:

1. Go to import/ export
2. Export to SIM card
3. Export to SD card or
4. Export to USB

Contact groups

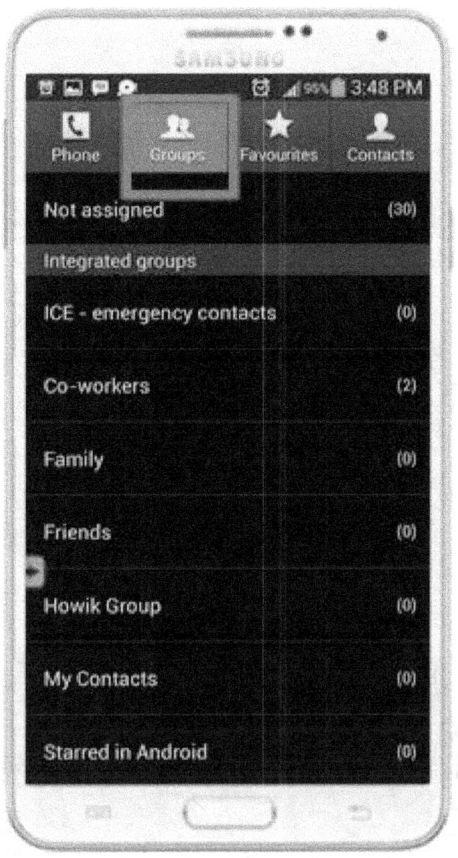

Add contacts to group:

1. Tap + after selecting a group
2. Select contacts to add
3. Tap done to complete action

Note: You can create multiple groups, search for contacts in a group, change the order of groups and delete groups as desired

Making and receiving calls

Tap **Phone** on Applications Screen to make or answer calls.

You can make calls through the keypad, logs, favorites, or contacts.

Speed Dial

Tap and hold the corresponding digit for speed dial numbers

To Find a Contact

1. To find contact in contact list, type the name, number or email address.
2. Predicted contacts will appear as characters are entered. To place a call, select one.

To Make an International Call

1. Until the plus sign appears, tap and hold 0.
2. Enter the country code, area code and phone number to place a call by tapping

To Add Contact

Enter number on keypad and tap Add to contacts

To Answer a Call

Drag the green phone icon out of the circle when a call comes in

To Reject a Call

Drag the red colored call icon out of the circle when a call comes in

To Reject A Call Automatically

Go to call   setting   call rejection   auto reject mode   auto reject numbers
auto reject list

Tap create to enter number and assign category

Tap save to enable the function

To Enable Call Waiting

Go to call ⟶ settings ⟶ additional settings ⟶ select call waiting

Note: to be able to use this service, check with your service provider

To Enable Call Forwarding

1. Go to call ⟶ settings ⟶ additional settings ⟶ call forwarding
2. Select call type and condition
3. Enter number and tap Enable

Music

To play a song, select a music category and play.

To open the music player screen, tap the album image at the bottom of the screen

To Set A Song As Ringtone

Go to set as and tap phone ringtone

To Share The Song

Go to play via group play

How to Create Playlists

1. Tap playlists
2. Go to create playlists
3. Enter title and tap ok
4. Select songs to add after tapping Add music
5. Tap done to finish

Play Music by Mood:

1. Go to settings ⟶ music menu ⟶ music square ⟶ tap done
2. The music square menu will appear on top of music library
3. The device automatically creates the playlist and plays music grouped by mood.
4. Select a mood cell by tapping music square at the top of screen.

Transfer Files

The files which are supported for transfer between the PC and Samsung Note 3 are:

Music: mp3, m4a, mp4, 3gp, 3ga, wma, ogg, oga, aac, and flac

Image: bmp, gif, jpg, and png

Video: avi, wmv, asf, flv, mkv, mp4, 3gp, webm and ts

Documents: doc, docx, xls, xlsx, ppt, pptx, pdf, and txt

You can transfer files in three ways:

Connect with Samsung Kies

1. Download Samsung Kies to manage media content from the Samsung website.
2. Connect using USB cable transfer files between device and computer.

Connect with windows media player

1 Sync music files by connecting the device via USB cable.
2 Open windows media player and start sync.

Connect as media device

1 Connect device via USB cable
2 From the notifications panel, select **Connected as media device ⟶ media device (MTP)**
3 Transfer files as usual

Messaging

You can send text or multimedia messages through your device

The format to send text messages is the same as on any other device.

Send Handwritten Messages

1   An icon appears at upper left corner of text field when you place the S Pen over the text field.

2   Tap the icon and then tap to enter and send a handwritten message

Send Scheduled Message

1   You can send a scheduled message by tapping **Scheduling**.

2   Set time and date

3   Tap **Done**

4   The message will be sent by the device at the set time and date

Note: your message will not be sent in case your phone is switched off, is not connected to a network or the network is not working properly.

Email

You can send and view emails on your device by tapping **Email** on the applications screen

Set Up an Account

When you open **Email** for the first time, you will have to set up an email account

1   Enter email address and password.

2   To set up private email account like Google, tap **Next**

3   To set up company email account tap **Manual Setup**

4   To complete the setup follow on screen instructions

Note: you can add other email accounts by going to ☰ ⟶ **settings** ⟶ **add account**

Send a Scheduled Email Message

1   Tap scheduled email and tick the box.

2   Set time and date

3   Tap done to complete action.

Internet

Tap **Internet** on applications screen for browsing

View WebPages

Enter web address in address field and tap **Go**

To Share or Print Current Webpage Tap

Tap address field, and tap search engine icon next to web address to change the search engine

To Open New Page

Tap ▤ ⟶ **new window**

Tap ▱ to go to another page and tap the page to select it

Camera

Tap **Camera** on applications screen to take photos or videos

Take a photo

1 Tap image for the camera to focus on preview screen

2 The focus frame will turn green when subject is in focus

3 Tap camera icon to take photo

Gallery

Tap **Gallery** on Applications screen to view images and videos

View Images

Available folders are displayed by launching Gallery

Images saved from other applications like Email are saved in the **Downloads** folder

Screenshots captured are saved in the **Screenshots** folder

To zoom in an image

Tap twice in a row on screen anywhere

Spread two fingers apart anywhere on screen

To zoom out an image

To zoom out, pinch or double-tap

PART 2

TIPS AND TRICKS FOR SAMSUNG NOTE 3

Reduce Battery Consumption

The device can be used longer between charges by deactivating features in the background and customizing options that help save battery.

1. Deactivate auto-syncing of applications
2. Deactivate Bluetooth when not in use
3. Deactivate Wi-Fi when not in use
4. Decrease screen brightness
5. Decrease time of back light
6. Switch to sleep mode by pressing the Power button when device is not in use

7. Using the task manager, close unnecessary applications

Replacing the S Pen Nib

You can replace the nib of the S Pen when it gets dull with a new one.

1. Pull the nib out gently by holding it with a tweezer

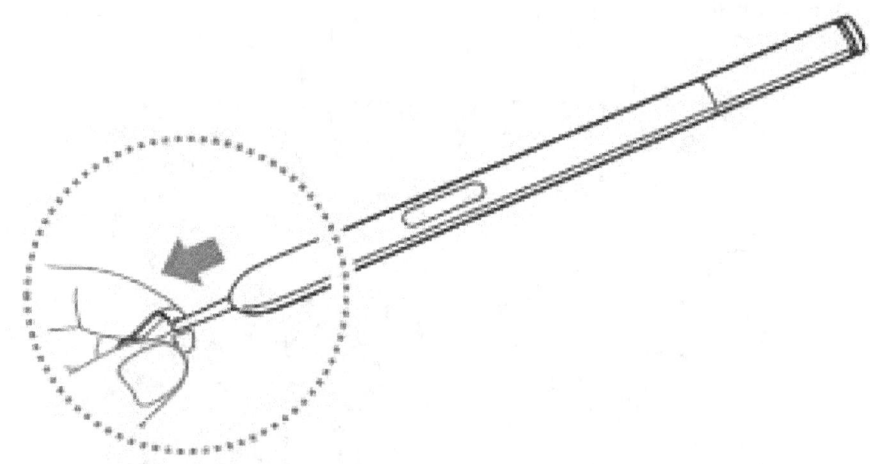

2. Insert the new nib until you hear a click.

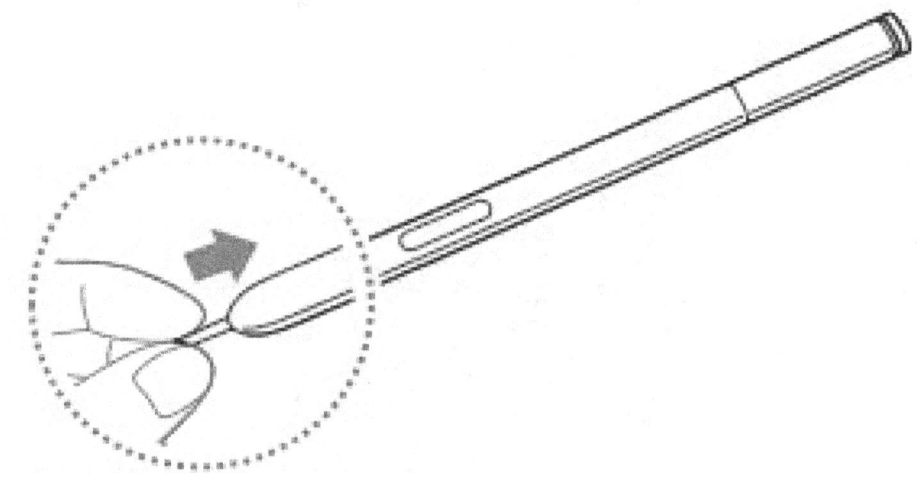

Enable Multi Window Mode

Using this feature you can run two applications at the same time on the screen.

To enable:

Tap Settings ⟶ Device ⟶ Multi Window

Note: applications on the Multi Window panel can run only

Using the Multi Window Panel

Tap and hold the back button to show the multi window panel. The panel appears at left side of screen.

1. Open the multi window tray by tapping

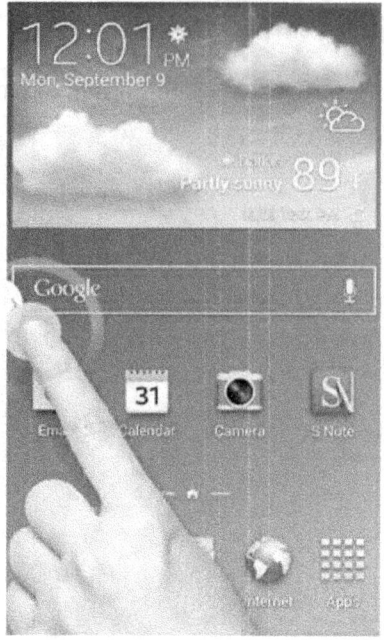

2. To open an application in a multi window screen, touch and drag it outside the tray. The appearance of window is indicated by a blue overlay.

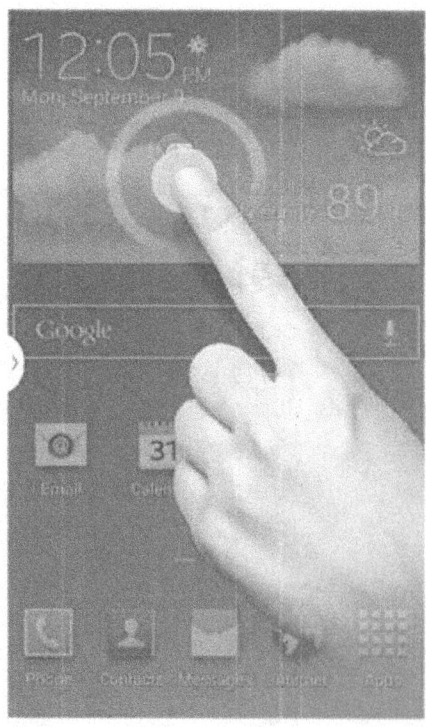

3. Touch and drag an application outside of the tray with the multi window tray open, to launch a side-by-side view

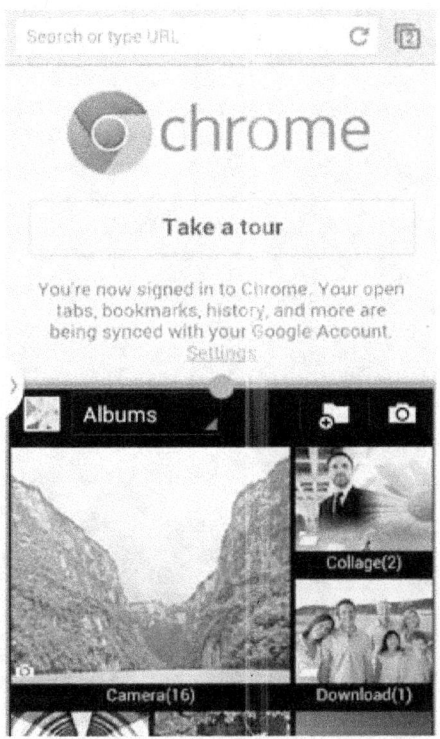

4. Tap and hold the back button again to hide the multi window panel.

Pen window

Using a pen window will enhance the functionality of the Mult-window feature of your device. It allows you to open apps in their window on top of the current location. You must activate Air command to use Pen window

Go to Menu ⟶ Settings ⟶ controls ⟶ Air command ⟶ and turn the slider on.

Hold the S Pen approximately 1.5 to 2.5 inches above the screen, and press and hold the button on the S Pen. The Air command controller should open.

1. Select Pen window

2. In the area you want the pen window to display, draw a rectangle

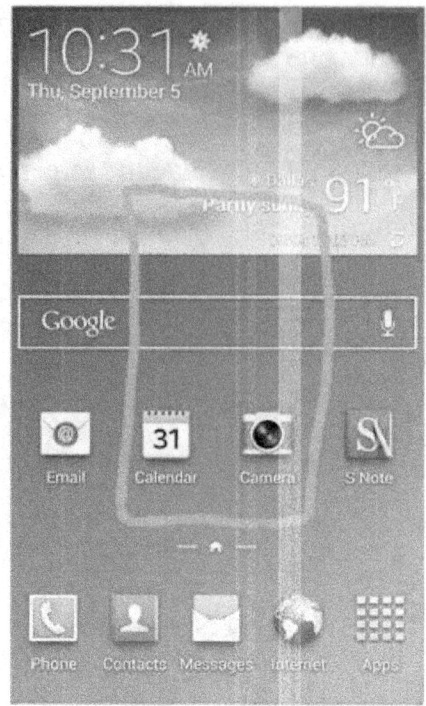

3. Select the app you want to open

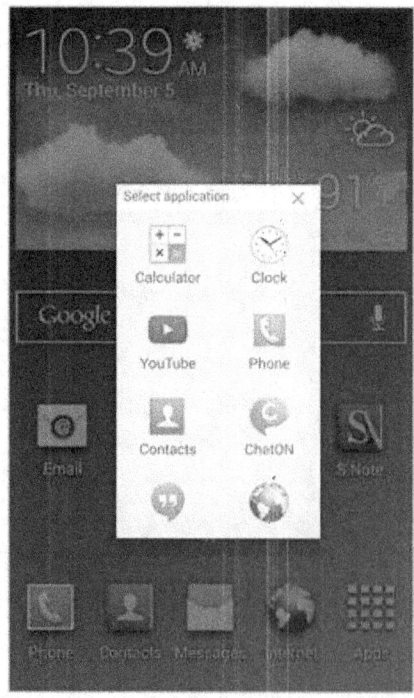

4. You can use the app normally as you otherwise would. You can touch the top of the window with the S Pen and move it around the screen.

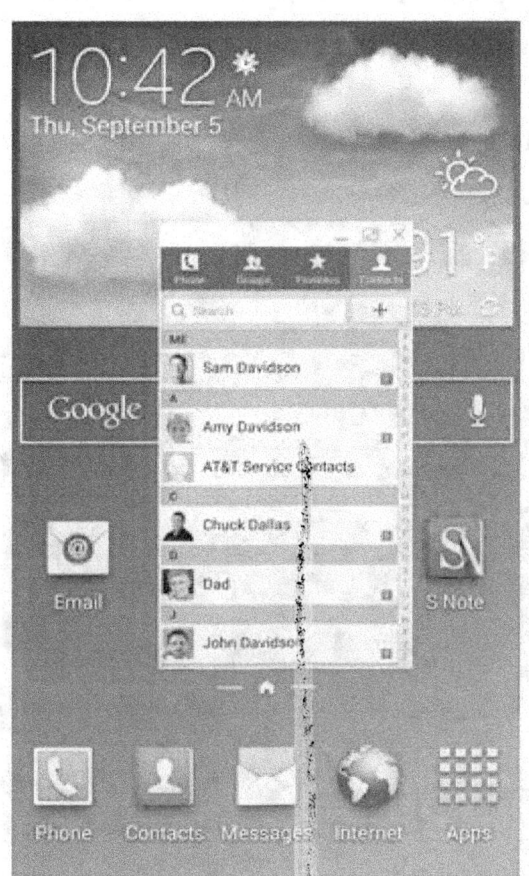

S Finder

Never lose your S Pen. The Samsung Note 3 alerts you when your S Pen isn't safely tucked inside its slot. To enable this feature:

Go to Settings ⟶ Controls ⟶ S Pen⟶ tick the box for S Pen Keeper

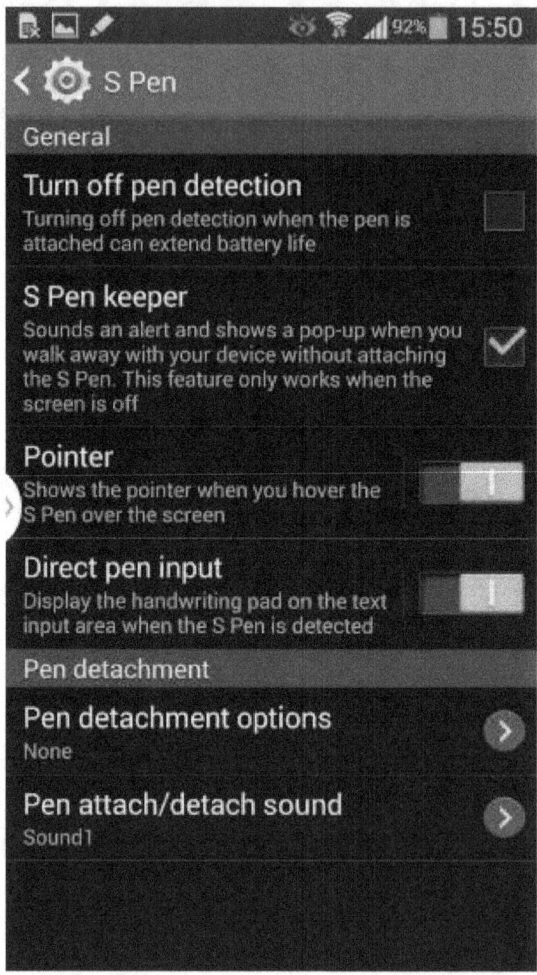

Air Gesture

Air gesture enables you to control functions without touching the screen

To activate:

Tap Apps ⟶ Settings ⟶ Controls ⟶ Air gesture ⟶ drag switch to right

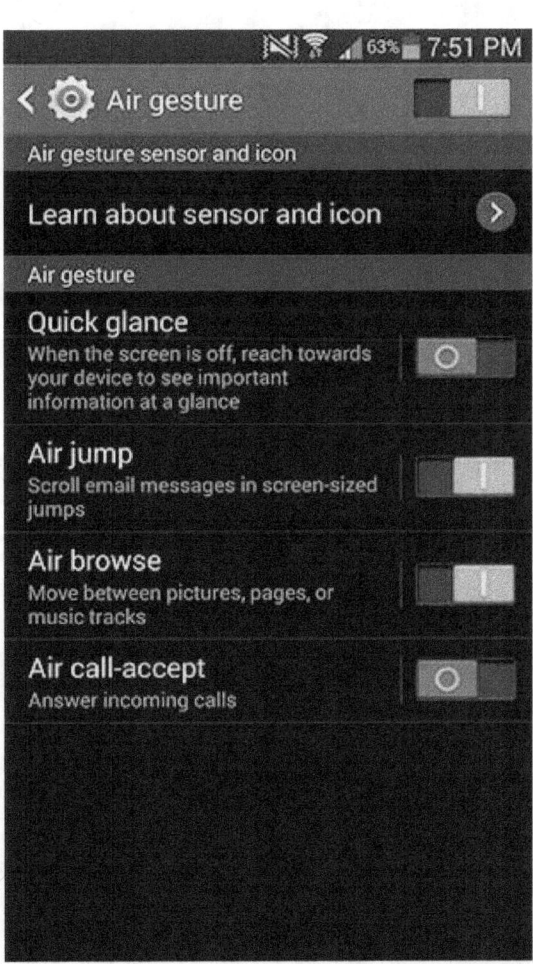

Quick Glance

Move your hand above the sensor to view notifications when the screen is off.

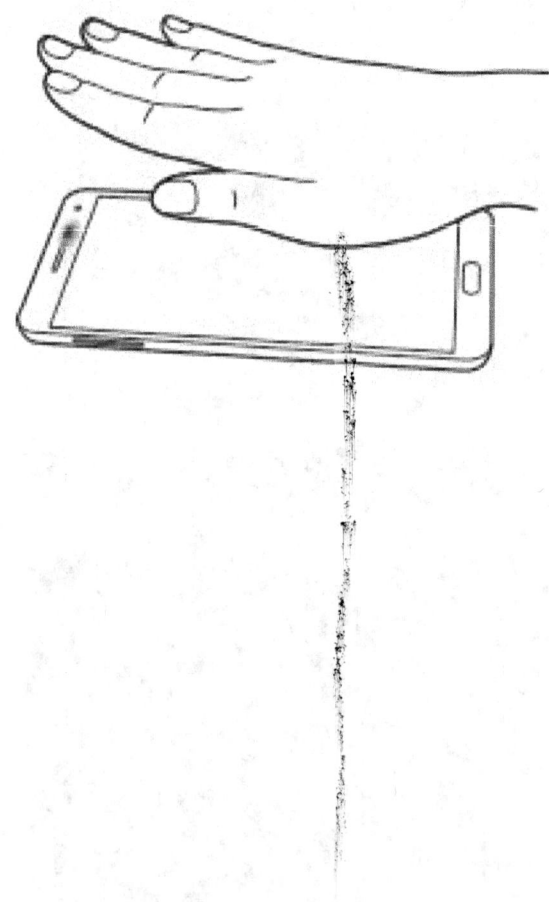

Air Jump

Move your hand up or down across sensor to scroll the page up or down while viewing emails or web pages.

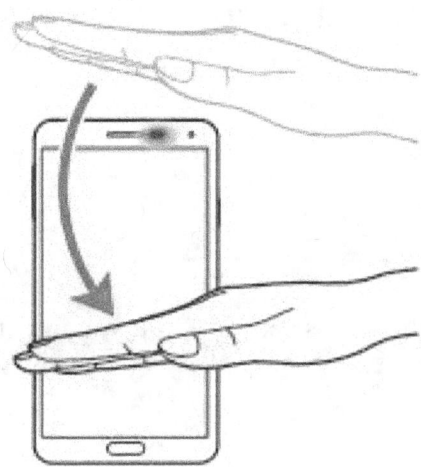

Air Browse

To browse images, web pages or songs, move your hand left or right across the sensor

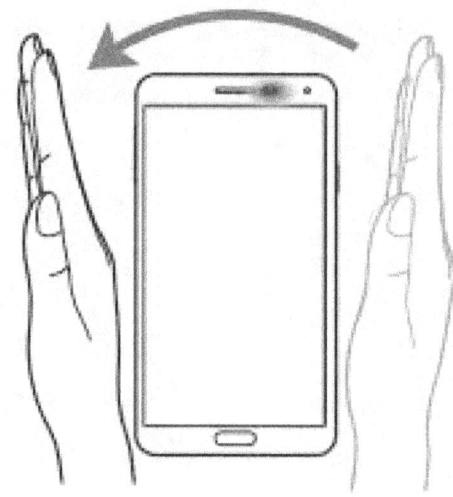

Air Move

Move your hand to the left or right across sensor while you tap and hold an app with the other hand, to move the icon to another location.

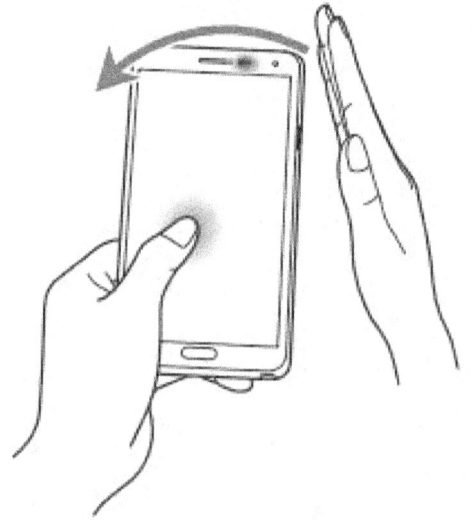

Air Call Accept

Move your hand to the left and then to the right across centre when a call comes in, to answer it.

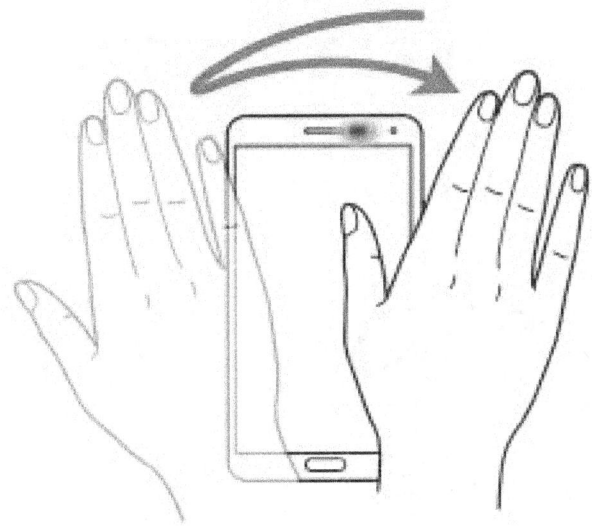

Palm Motions

To control device by touching the screen, use palm motions. To activate the feature:

Tap Apps ⟶ Settings ⟶ Controls ⟶ Palm motion ⟶ drag switch to right

Sweeping

To capture a screen shot, sweep your hand across screen. Go to Gallery ⟶ Screenshots to view saved images.

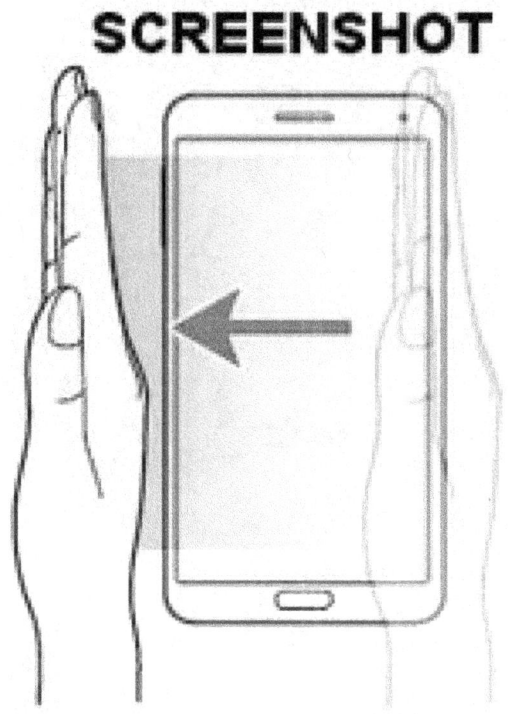

Covering

To pause media playback, cover screen with palm

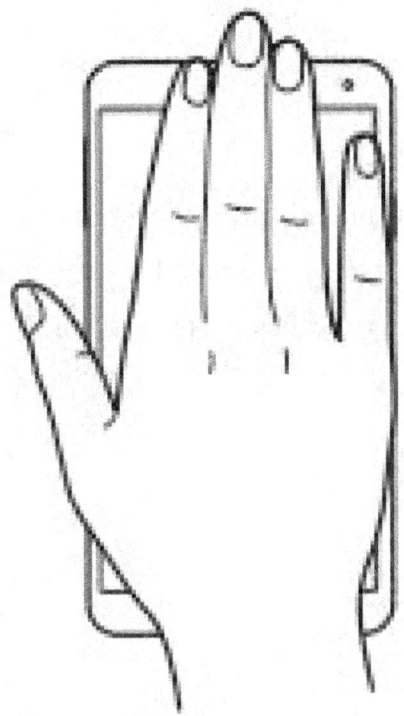

Switching Device to Silent Mode

You can switch device to silent by:

1 Pressing and holding volume button until it switched to silent mode
2 Tap Mute or Vibrate after you press and hold Power button
3 Tap Sound or Vibrate from the notifications panel at the top of screen

CONTROL MOTION TRICKS

When you enable Motions from the Control settings you are able to do the following:

Pick Up Device

Your device will vibrate if you have missed calls or new messages, when you pick it up after some time of it staying idle.

Panning to Browse

Tap and hold a point on screen when an image is zoomed in, and you can browse the image by moving the device in any direction

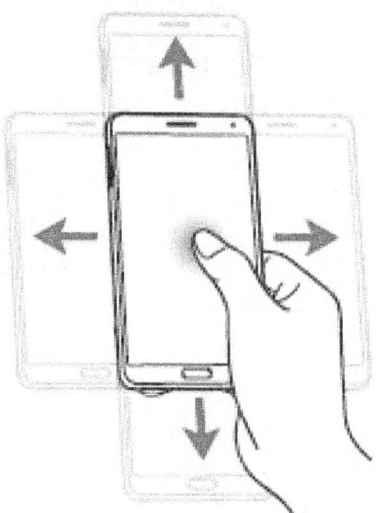

Tilt

Tilt the device back and forth after you tap and hold any two points on the screen, to zoom in or zoom out.

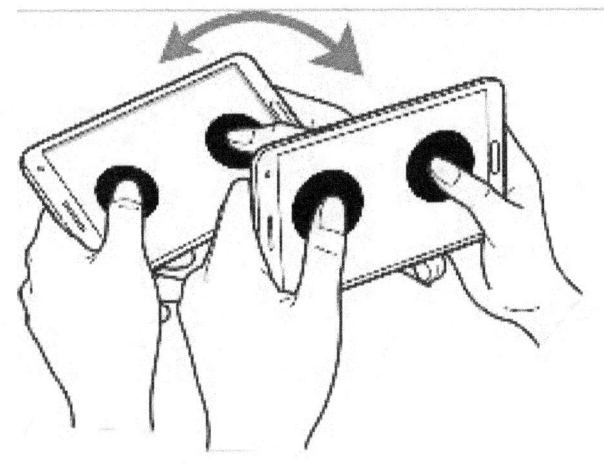

Turn Over

To mute ringtone or pause media playback, turn over the device

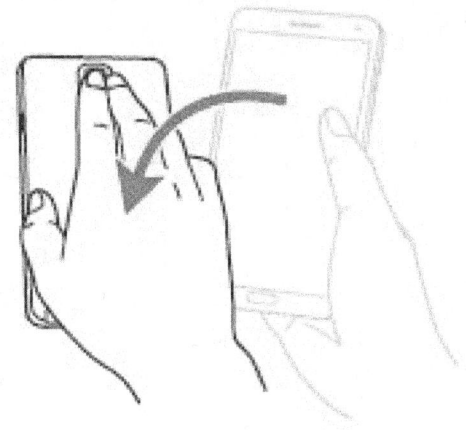

Smart Pause

With this feature, you can pause videos when you look away from screen

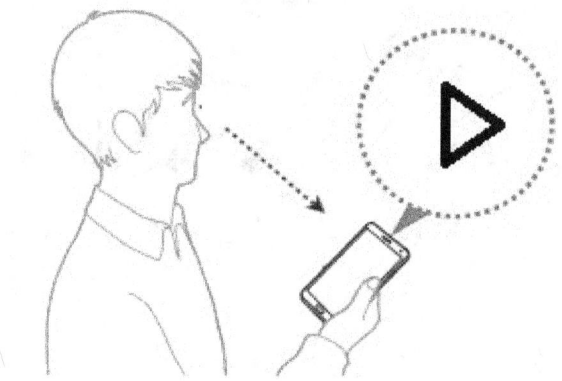

To enable:

Tap Apps ⟶ Settings ⟶ Controls ⟶ Smart Screen ⟶ tick Smart Pause

The video will play again as you look back at the screen

Smart Stay

Keep your Note 3 display from going blank when you are using it by enabling **Smart Stay**

Go to Settings ⟶ Controls ⟶ Smart Screen ⟶ Smart Stay ⟶ drag switch to right

Smart Scroll

With his feature you can scroll the screen by tilting either head or the device

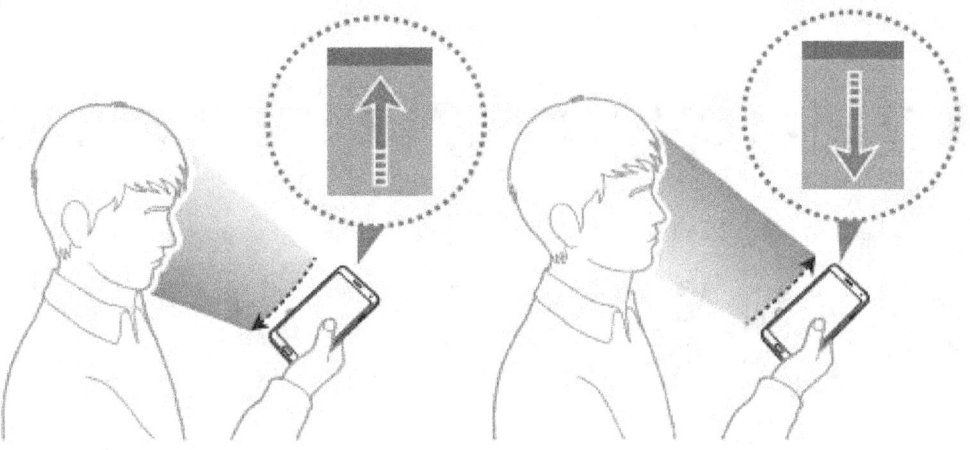

To enable:

Tap Apps ⟶ Settings ⟶ Controls ⟶ Smart Screen ⟶ Smart Scroll ⟶ drag switch to right

Easy Mode

To enable:

Tap settings ⟶ device ⟶ easy mode ⟶ drag switch to right

This feature simplifies the use of Note 3, making it user friendly for first time users

One Handed Operation

This mode modifies application interfaces for easy use.

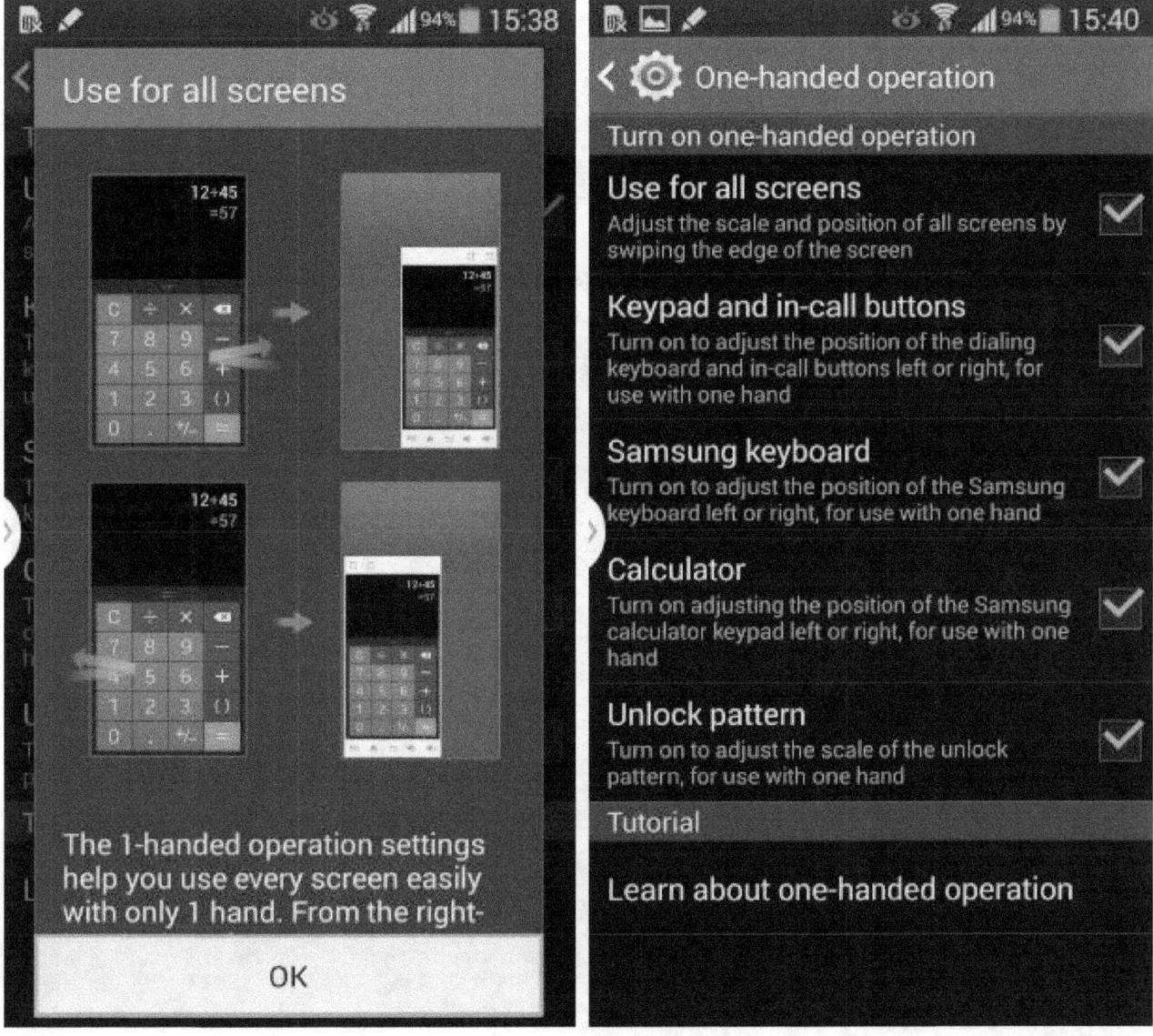

To enable:

1 Tap Settings ⟶ controls ⟶ one-handed operations

2   Select the features to use with the mode

HOW TO SECURE THE DEVICE

Enhance device security using this feature

How To Set A Signature

Tap settings ──► device ──► lock screen ──► screen lock ──► signature

You will have to draw the signature three times with your S Pen for verifications

You Can Also Set Up A Back Up PIN To Unlock Device When You Forget The Signature

Set A Pattern

Tap settings ──► device ──► lock screen ──► screen lock ──► pattern

Draw pattern twice for verification by connecting four or more dots.

How To Set A Pin

Tap settings ──► device ──► lock screen ──► screen lock ──► PIN

To set up PIN you will have to enter at least four numbers

Set A Password

Tap settings ──► device ──► lock screen ──► screen lock ──► password

Include numbers and symbols to set at least a four character password

Increase Sensitivity Of Touch Screen

You can increase the devices touch screen sensitivity by:

Tap Apps ——→ settings ——→ controls ——→ tick box next to **Increase Touch Sensitivity**

This will enable you to operate the touch screen wearing gloves

Enable Camera Flash For Call Alert

Tap settings ——→ device——→ accessibility ——→ check box next to **flash notification**

This feature will alert you for incoming calls

Enable Hands Free Mode

To enable:

Tap settings ——→ controls ——→ enable **hands free mode**

Pick the features you prefer

Adjust The Display And Sound

Turning on **modify display** will modify the color variety saturation and sharpness for various apps like camera gallery and play books

To enable:

Tap Settings ⟶ device ⟶ display ⟶ screen mode ⟶ adapt display

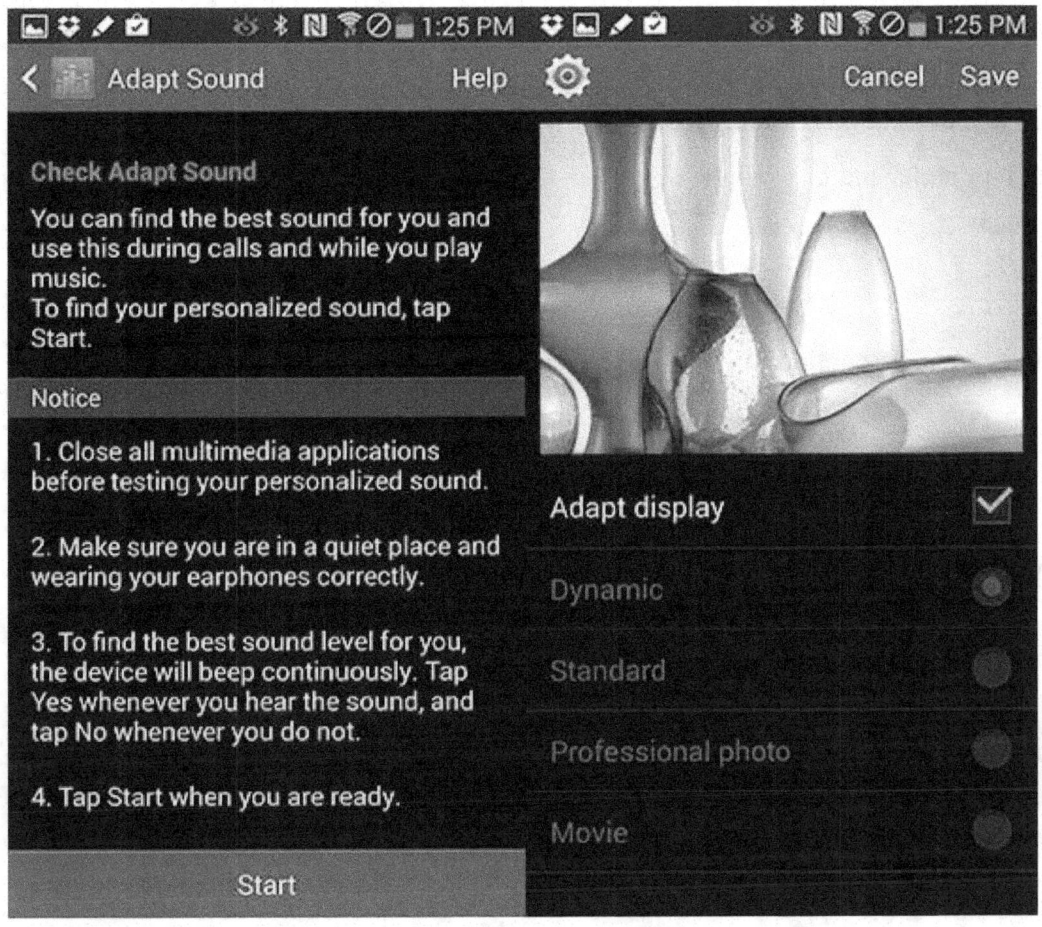

Consequently to modify sound

Tap settings ⟶ device ⟶ sound ⟶ adapt sound start

Enable Battery Percentage In Status Bar

To view the battery status in percentage

Tap settings ⟶ device ⟶ display ⟶ check box against **display battery percentage**

NFC

Red near field communication tags that contain product information through this feature. You can make payments and buy tickets also.

To activate:

Tap settings ⟶ connections ⟶ NFC ⟶ drag switch to right

S Beam

Send data such as videos and documents through this feature

To enable:

Tap settings ⟶ connections ⟶ S Beam ⟶ drag switch to right

Select file and place the back of devices together and tap screen of your device

INTERNET TIPS AND TRICKS

Bookmarks

Tap  ⟶ **Add bookmarks**

Enter title and tap **Save**

History

Tap history to open recently visited webpage

Tap ᵈ⊞ ⟶ **clear history** to clear

Links

To open link in a new page, save it or copy, tap and hold the link

Use **Downloads** to view saved links

Share webpages

Tap ▤ ⟶ share via to share webpage address with others

Tap and hold desired text and tap Share via to share part of a webpage

Screen Mirroring

You can connect your device to a large screen with AllShare Cast dongle or Home Sync and share content.

To enable:

1 Tap settings connections screen mirroring
2 Select the device and open or play file
3 You can control the display with the keys on the device

How To Enable Bluetooth

Tap settings ⟶ connections ⟶ Bluetooth ⟶ drag switch to right

How To Disable Auto Pen Input

Tap settings ⟶ Samsung keyboard ⟶ uncheck pen detection

Using Gesture Typing

Use gesture typing on virtual keyboard to create fast text for messaging or email

Tap settings ⟶ controls ⟶ language and input ⟶ Samsung keyboard ⟶ keyboard swipe ⟶ continuous input

Control Your Television

Tap WatchON from the applications screen to enable control of your television through the device.

Make sure the device is connected to a network and the infrared port is facing the television

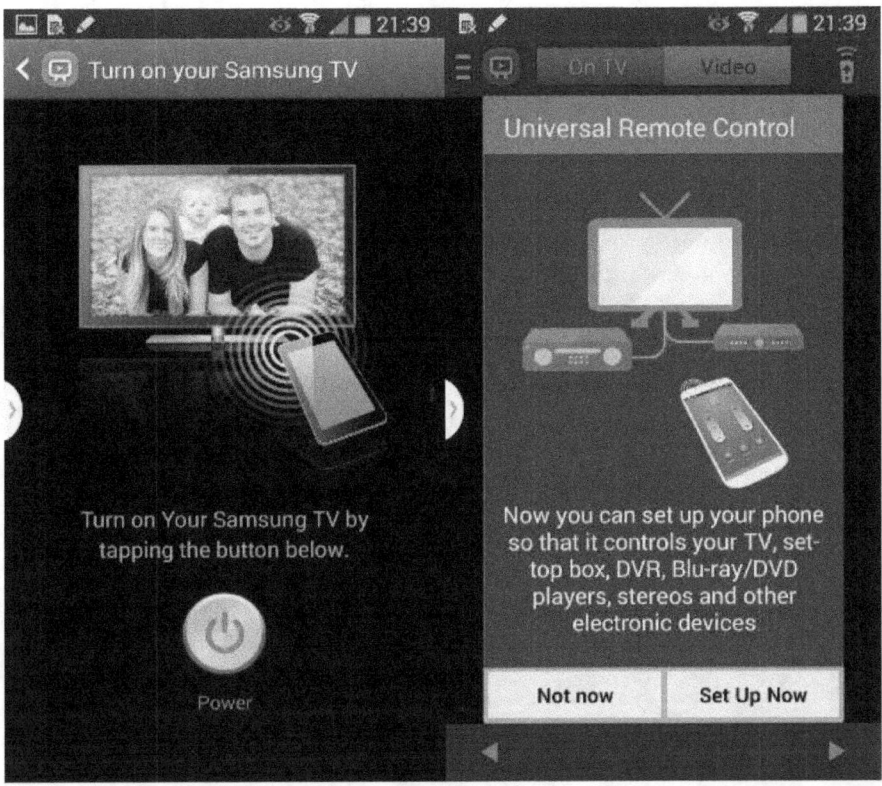

Set A Programme Reminder

1   Select time for the TV programme you want to watch by tapping time at bottom of screen.

2   Select programme and tap Reminder.

3   Set an alarm time and you are done.

Haptic Feedback

Functions that respond through haptic feedback can drain battery

Tap settings ⟶ sound ⟶ Haptic feedback ⟶ drag switch to left

Control Music Player With Voice Control

You can activate the feature of voice control for music player and control it using your voice through commands like play or pause

Tap settings ⟶ controls ⟶ voice control to enable.

Creating A Personalized Wallpaper

You can personalize your own wallpaper for the home screen. An image with a resolution of 1920 into 1080 is recommended to be used.

Go to gallery select image and tap pencil icon

USB 3.0

You can transfer files quickly using a USB cable. The device supports a 3.0 port also along with a 2.0 USB port.

Home Cinema

You can turn your phone into a home cinema by connecting it to the television via a HDMI cable.

View Recently Used Apps

Press and hold the home key to display recently used apps

How To Enable Lock Screen Shortcuts

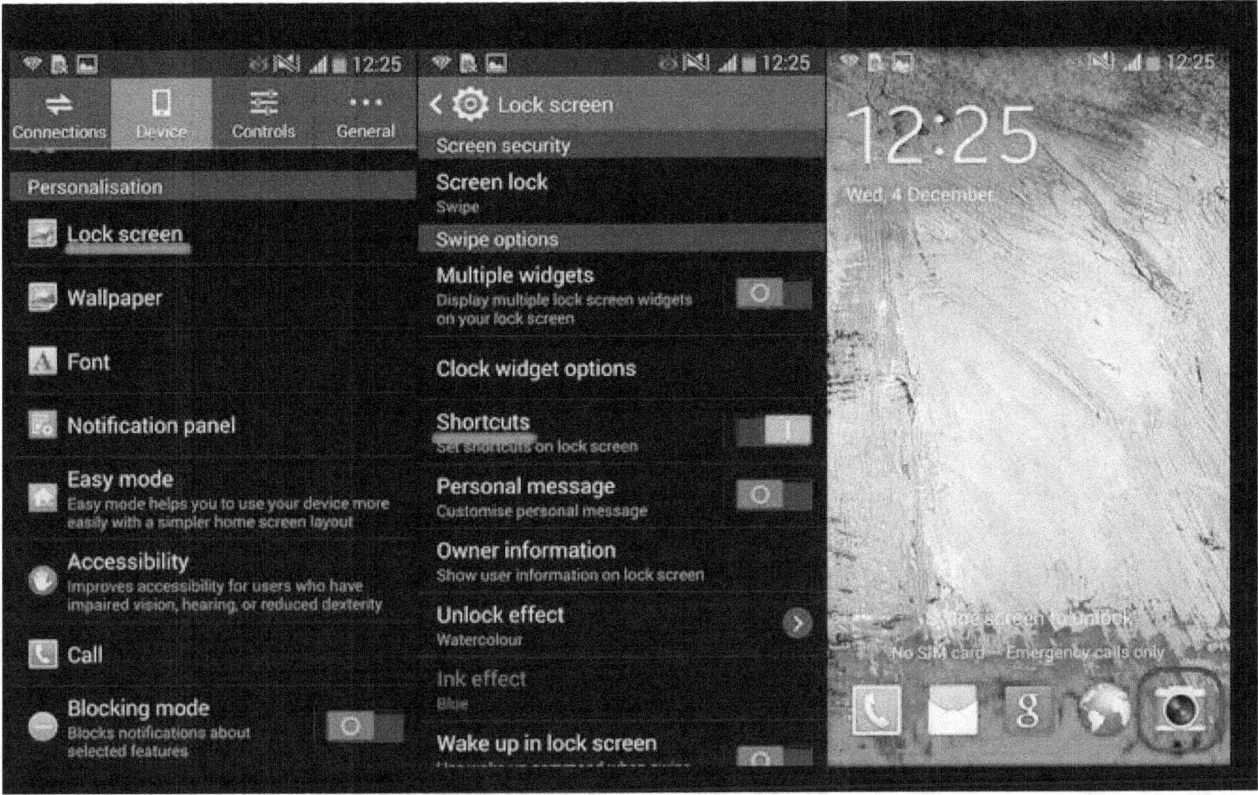

Go to settings ⟶ lock screen menu

CAMERA TIPS AND TRICKS

Dual Camera Mode

You can take a landscapre photo and self portrait simultaneously using this feature

To enable:

Tap ⬚

Share Shot

Tap settings on camera screen and tap the sharing icon to share photos

Trim Video Segments

1   Select video and tap the scissor like icon.
2   Set the desired starting and ending point of the brackets ro get the desired video length

Favorite Images

Tap ⬚ ⟶ **favorite** to add image to favorites list

Make An Image Collage

Tap ⬚ ⟶ select item in a folder.

Select two to four images

Tap ⬚ ⟶ **create collage**

At the bottom of screen select a style and tap **save**

Set Image As Wallpaper

Tap ⟶ **Set as** to assign image to contact or set as wallpaper image

Share Images

Tap ⟶ **select item**

Select desired images and tap share icon

Tag Faces In An Image

Tap ⟶ **settings** and tick face tag

Around the face a yellow frame will appear

Tap face and tap add name

Use Tag Buddy

Tap ⟶ settings ⟶ tag buddy drag switch to right

Organize Images With Folders

1   To create a new folder tap

2   Enter folder name and tap OK and tick the desired images or videos

3   Tap and hold the selected images to drag to new folder

4   Tap **Done** to finish

Story Album

Create your own digital album with this feature

Tap **Story Album** and install it

How to Create a Story Album

Select images from gallery and tap plus icon

Select an option

Use The Right Camera Resolution

By default your phone will shoot photos with 9.6MP with an aspect ratio of 16:9. Improve it to 13MP at 4:3 to save storage space and improve pictures

Use Volume Key As Camera Shutter

By default the volume key controls the digital zoom level. You can change the option and use it as a shutter

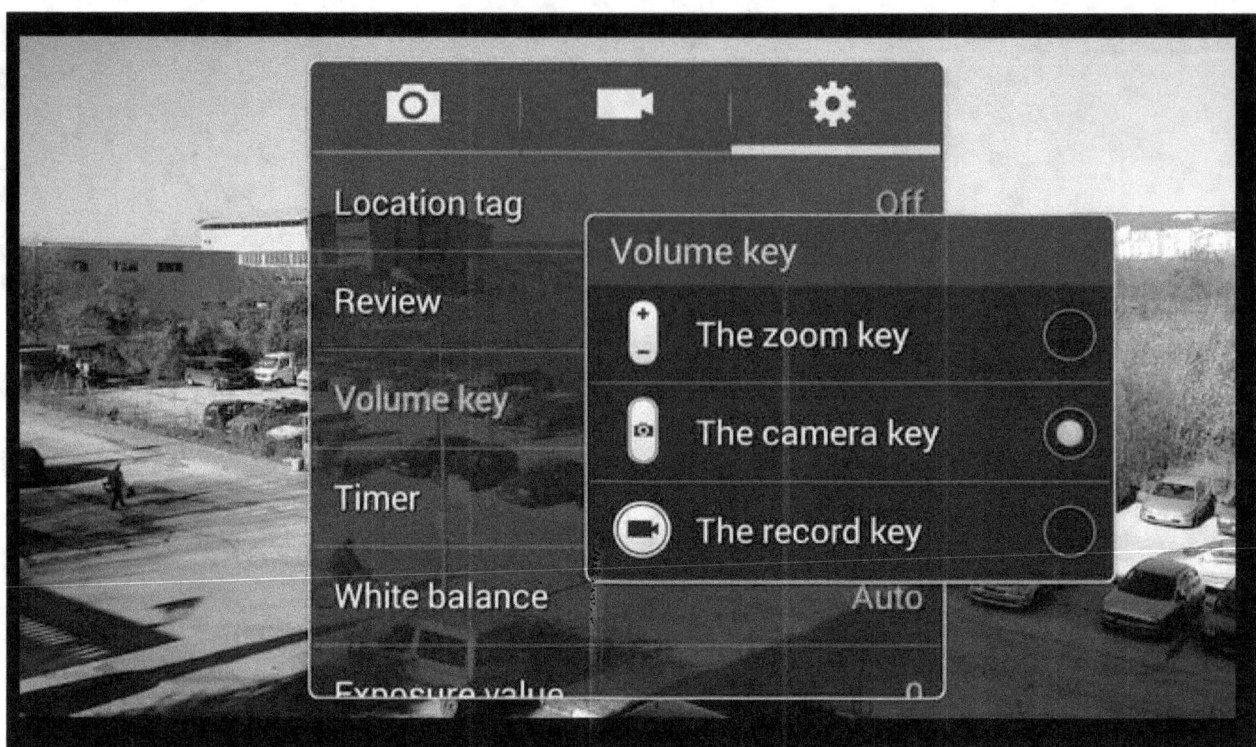

Lock The Focus In Videos

Hold the area you want to focus until an AF button appears on the screen. Until you tap on the button, the focus will remain locked.

My magazine

You can make your own social magazine with this application.

Tap ▤ to set up your magazine and tick the categories

Tap right side facing arrow to select new topics and then tap backward facing arrow

To change categories flick right or left, to turn magazine pages flick up or down.

Flipboard

You can access your personalized magazines through this application

1 Tap build your flipboard to start it,
2 Flick on greetings page and select new topics
3 Select an article to read by selecting a cover story and flicking through flipboard pages

Mute Phone With Your Palm

Place your palm over the sensor to mute your phone while screen is on

Tap Settings ⟶ controls ⟶ palm motion

Sketchbook

Tap **sketchbook** for Galaxy to create a quick sketch of your idea

The image is saved in Gallery

Bloomberg+

You can tap Bloomberg+ to access latest news about finance, business and more

Take Smart Notes

You can take a quick note without having to unlock your phone

Tap settings ⟶ device ⟶ lock screen ⟶ check the box next to **Action memo** on lock screen

Double tap S Pen on lock screen while holding the button on the stylus to take the note.

Search Quickly

Use the S Finder to quickly find a document or image.

You can bring up the S Finder by long pressing the menu button.

Block Notifications While Sleeping

You can choose who can disturb you and block unwanted notifications and calls while in a meeting or while sleeping.

To enable

Tap the feature on from notifications tray

You can set an automatic start and stop time for blocking mode from settings

Unlock Phone Through Voice Control

With the voice control mode on, you can control your device even when it is asleep. Just say Hi Galaxy to enable S Voice and tell the phone what to do. You can make calls, send text messages and more.

To enable

Tap applications ⟶ voice menu ⟶ settings ⟶ tick box next to **Voice Wakeup**

View Notifications With Two Finger Pull

Pull down the notification bar with two finger and you will be able to see all settings toggles instead of pending notifications.

Using A USB Drive

You can store movies and other files for access on Note 3 using a USB drive with the device

The phone enables use of a Micro USB OTG cable to let you store a lot of files on your device

Enable Reading Mode

Tweak the screen for a better look for your eyes with the Reading Mode. This mode makes reading easier for long periods

Tap on the reading mode icon from notifications panel to enable.

Quick Message Or Call

To quick message or call simply swipe the contact left or right instead of tapping on it.

Take Incoming Calls In A Small Window

Tap settings ⟶ device ⟶ scroll to call ⟶ and check the box next to **incoming call notifications**

This will enable you to receive calls in a small pop up window rather than a full screen alert.

Change Lock Screen Effect

Tap settings ⟶ device ⟶ lock screen ⟶ unlock effect

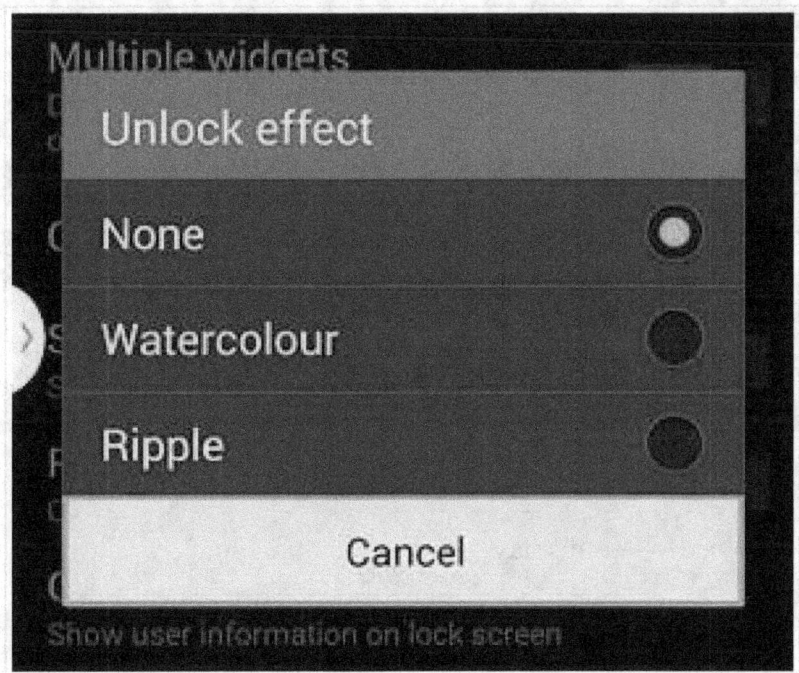

Select none watercolor or ripple to change the effect on lock screen.

Change Screen Timeout

You can customize the length of time before the screen turns off

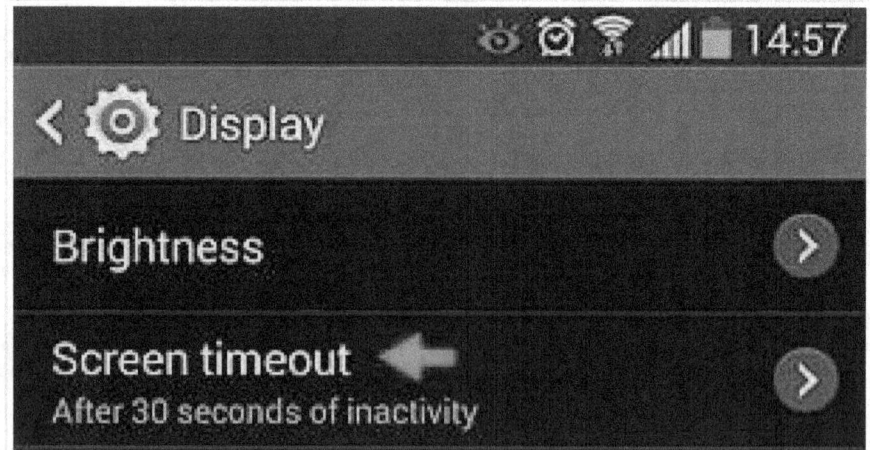

Tap settings⟶ device ⟶ display ⟶ screen timeout

Turn Screen Off During Call

To prevent accidental touches during a call

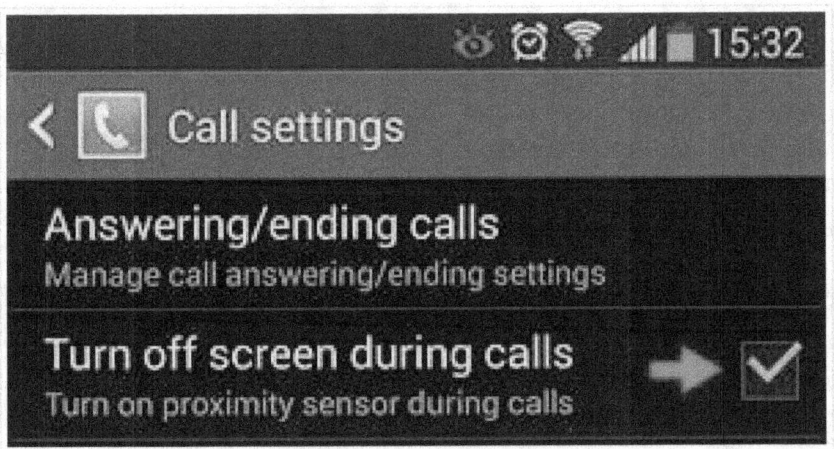

1   Tap settings⟶ device ⟶ call

2   Check the box next to **Turn off screen during calls**

How To Add Or Remove Home Screens

By default there are 5 home screen panels on Note 3. You can add or delete them as you like

1   Place two fingers on any panel and pinch them together to edit

2   Tap and hold the thumbnail of panel and drag to dustbin to remove

3   Tap the + sign to add a panel

Scrapbook

You can keep track of what you like using your very own digital scrapbook. Collect favorite articles pictures objects videos etc.

Reduce Vibration Intensity

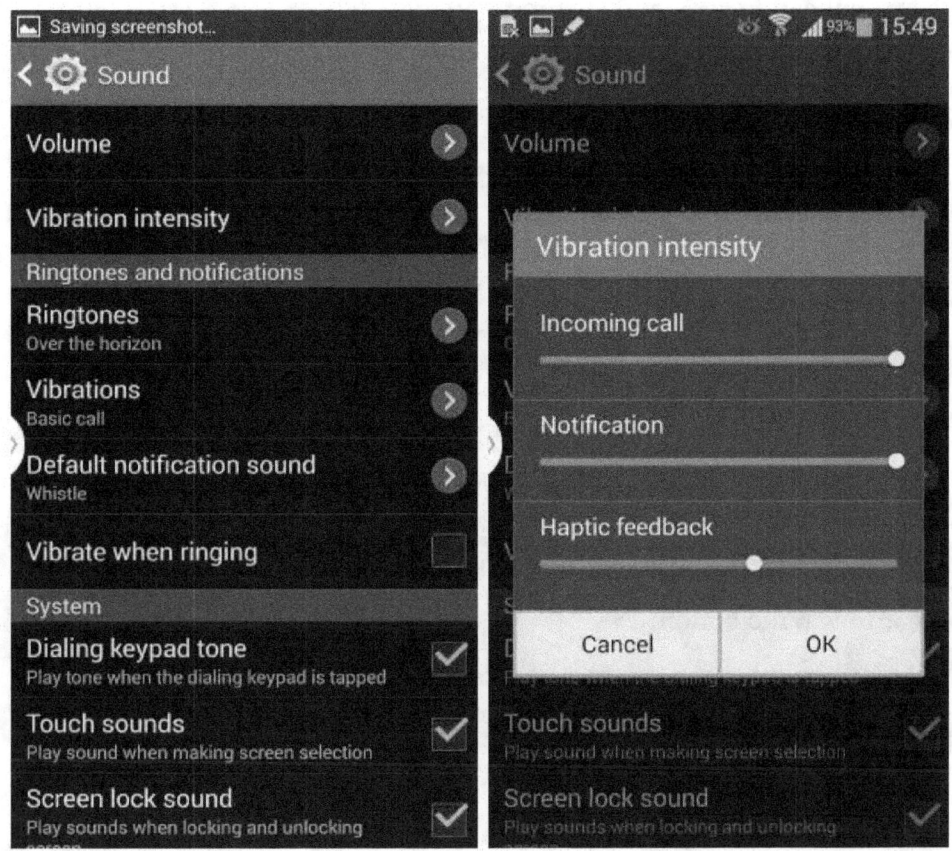

Tap settings device sound vibration intensity

Enter text by voice

Speak into microphone after activating voice input. The device will display what you speak. Tap underlined text for alternative word if it does not recognize what you speak.

Hangouts

Tap hangouts on application screen to chat with others

ChatON

To chat with any device, use this application.

You need to verify your number or sign in from a Samsung account.

Launch apps in pairs

1   Open two apps you like and would want to pair together
2   Scroll down to bottom of multiwindow panel
3   Tap the arrow at the bottom
4   Tap the icon showing two screen sections
5   The pair will be created

Monitor your usage of mobile data

Tap ——→ settings ——→ connections ——→ data usage

How to auto reject calls

Tap settings ——→ device call ——→ call rejection

How To Use Popup Video Player

Yu can use other application without having to close the video player

Tap the double video icon while watching videos to use the pop up player

Make Video Clips

Tap ▦ ⟶ in folder and tap **create video clips**

Select images by ticking and then tap the tick icon

Enter title select an option for effect and then tap save

Adding Widgets to Lock Screen

Tap apps ⟶ settings ⟶ device ⟶ lock screen ⟶ multiple widgets ⟶

drag switch to right

S Pen Popup Window: How to Remove It

To deactivate automatic launch of Air Command when taking out S Pen

Tap settings ⟶ control ⟶ S Pen ⟶ Pen detachment option ⟶ none

Customize Quick Settings Buttons on Notification Panel

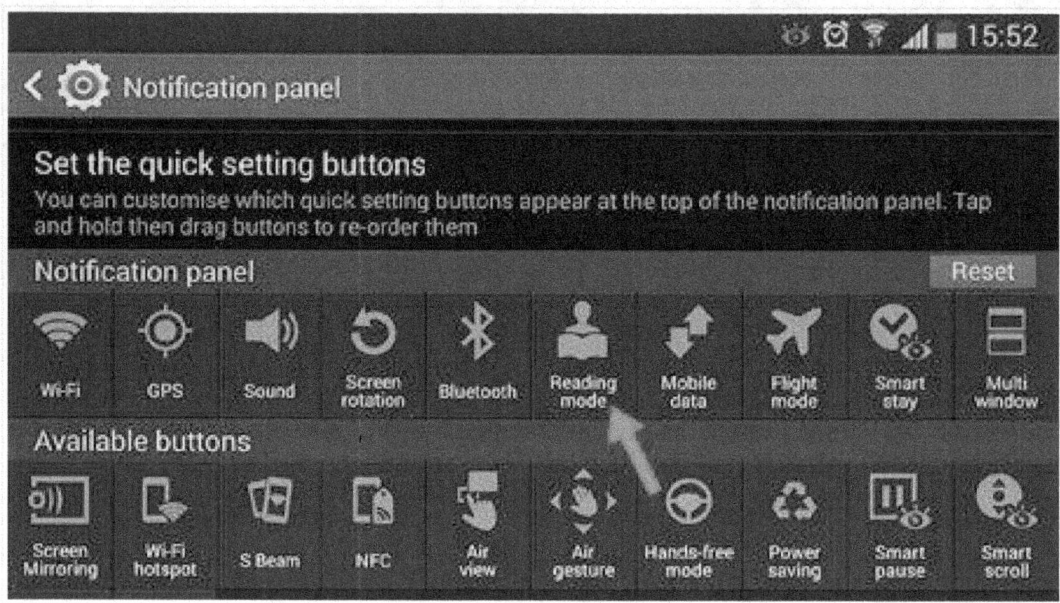

Tap settings ⟶ device ⟶ notification panel

Tap and drag buttons from available options to add or replace unwanted buttons.